Contents

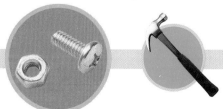

Looking at buildings

⭐ Draw or paint a picture of a house.

⭐ Cut out the labels on Task Sheet 1. Stick them on your picture.

Scientific Enquiry

Materials in your home

bedroom

bathroom

kitchen

living room

✺ Be a materials spotter.

✺ What materials can you spot in the classroom?

✺ Take Task Sheet 2 home with you.

✺ Look in each room.
How many materials can you spot?

✺ Write them on Task Sheet 2.

✺ Share your answers with the class.

Building bricks

YOU NEED:

plastic brick

clay brick

wooden brick

✸ Look at these bricks.
What do they look like?

✸ Pick up each brick.

✸ Make a table like this.

Brick	What the brick is like
Clay	hard, rough, heavy
Plastic	
Wooden	

✸ Describe the bricks. Use some of these words

hard   light   rough

shiny   cold   dull   soft

warm   smooth   heavy

4

Making bricks

❈ Make your own set
of small bricks.

❈ What materials could
you use?

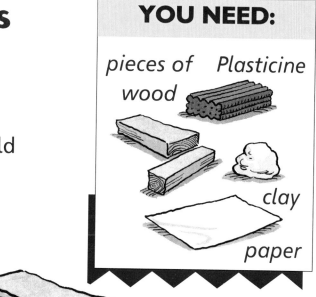

YOU NEED:

pieces of   Plasticine
wood

clay

paper

Plasticine

pieces of wood

clay

❈ Make each brick.

❈ Put it on a piece of paper.

❈ Write words on the paper
to describe each brick.

smooth   heavy

The same material

✿ Collect some things from around the classroom.

✿ Sort them into sets of the same material.

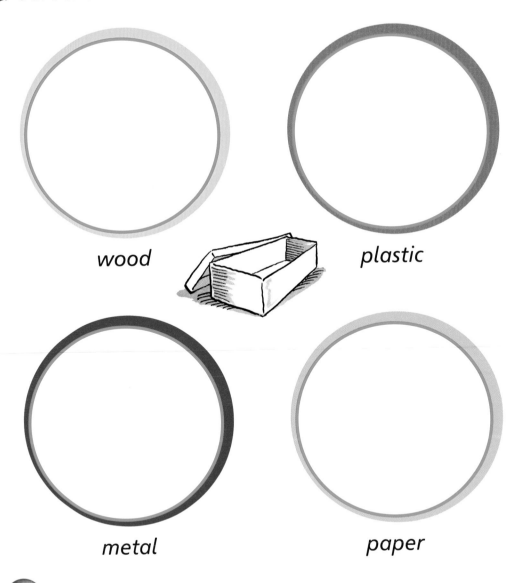

wood

plastic

metal

paper

6 Facts about materials

✻ Look at the sets you made in Task 5.

✻ Choose one of them.

✻ Find out five facts about the material in your set.

✻ Write your facts on Task Sheet 3.

✻ Share your facts with others in your class.

Different materials

✿ Find some materials that are transparent.

✿ Draw or list them on Task Sheet 4.

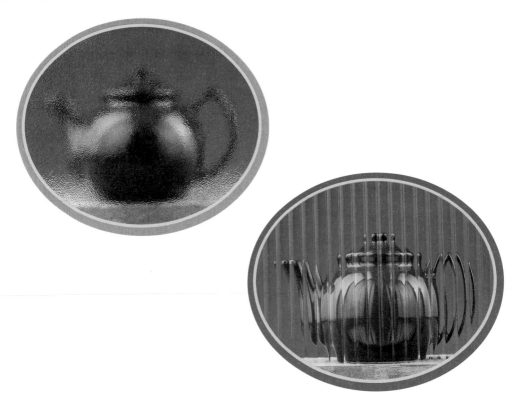

✿ Find some materials that are translucent.

✿ Draw or list them on Task Sheet 5.

Fuzzy windows

There are different
types of glass.
Some are translucent.

✦ Which rooms have
glass that is translucent?

✦ Complete Task Sheet 6.

Sorting wallpaper

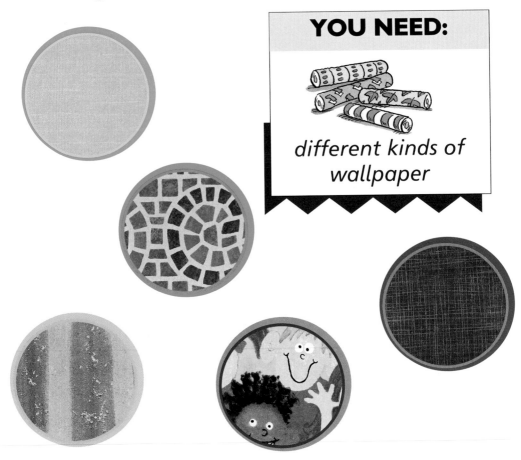

YOU NEED:

different kinds of wallpaper

⭐ What are the different kinds of wallpaper like? Do they look the same?

⭐ Sort them into groups.

⭐ How will you sort them?

Choosing wallpaper

☆ Choose four different kinds of wallpaper.

☆ Stick a piece of each one in the empty boxes on Task Sheet 7.

YOU NEED:

different kinds of wallpaper

☆ Now fill in the table on Task Sheet 7 like this.

Type of wallpaper	What the wallpaper is like
	stripy, smooth, shiny

11

Task 11 Waterproof materials

- Collect six objects made of different materials.

- Sort them into two sets.

- In one set put materials that you think are waterproof.

- In the other set put materials that you think are not waterproof.

waterproof

not waterproof

Task 12 Garden chairs

YOU NEED:

different materials

❋ What materials could you cover garden chairs with, to keep them dry when it rains?

❋ How could you find out?

❋ Collect some materials to test.

❋ Use Task Sheet 8 to help you plan your investigation.

❋ Record your results in a table.

Material	Is it waterproof?

❋ Use Task Sheet 9.

Marvellous magnets

Some materials stick to magnets.
They are called magnetic materials.

✴ Collect some magnets.

✴ Which materials are magnetic?

✴ Make a table like this one.

Material	Is it magnetic?
Wood	No

Fridge magnets

✴ How could you make
a fridge magnet?

✴ What things would you need?

✴ Make a list.

✴ Now make your
own fridge
magnet.

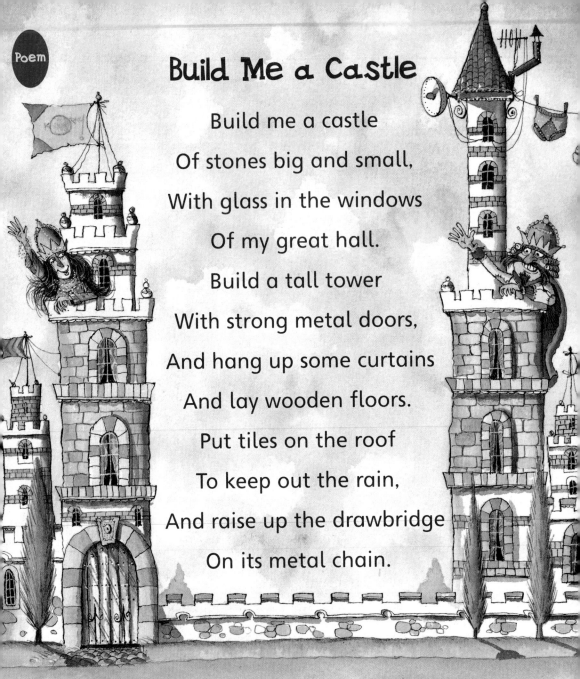

Build Me a Castle

Build me a castle

Of stones big and small,

With glass in the windows

Of my great hall.

Build a tall tower

With strong metal doors,

And hang up some curtains

And lay wooden floors.

Put tiles on the roof

To keep out the rain,

And raise up the drawbridge

On its metal chain.

✪ What materials are used to build the castle in this poem? Write what each material is like.